Keeping Healthy

Taking Care of My Skin

by Terri DeGezelle

Consulting Editor: Gail Saunders-Smith, PhD

Consultant: Amy Grimm, MPH
Program Director, National Center for Health Education
New York, New York

Capstone
press

Mankato, Minnesota

Pebble Plus is published by Capstone Press,
151 Good Counsel Drive, P.O. Box 669, Mankato, Minnesota 56002.
www.capstonepress.com

1 2 3 4 5 6 10 09 08 07 06 05

Library of Congress Cataloging-in-Publication Data
DeGezelle, Terri, 1955–
    Taking care of my skin / by Terri DeGezelle.
    p. cm.—(Pebble plus. Keeping healthy)
    Includes bibliographical references and index.
    ISBN 0-7368-4263-2 (hardcover)
    1. Skin—Care and hygiene—Juvenile literature. I. Title. II. Series.
RL87.D44 2006
646.7'26—dc22   2004026748

Summary: Simple text and photographs present ways to keep your skin healthy.

Editorial Credits
Sarah L. Schuette, editor; Jennifer Bergstrom, designer; Stacy Foster, photo resource coordinator

Photo Credits
Capstone Press/Karon Dubke, all

The author dedicates this book to Molly DeGezelle Willaert.

Note to Parents and Teachers

The Keeping Healthy set supports science standards related to physical health and life
skills for personal health. This book describes and illustrates how to take care of your
skin. The images support early readers in understanding the text. The repetition of words
and phrases helps early readers learn new words. This book also introduces early readers
to subject-specific vocabulary words, which are defined in the Glossary section. Early
readers may need assistance to read some words and to use the Table of Contents,
Glossary, Read More, Internet Sites, and Index sections of the book.

Table of Contents

My Amazing Skin

I use my skin to touch.
Nerves in my skin send
messages to my brain.

My brain understands

the messages.

Then I know

how something feels.

What My Skin Does

Skin covers and protects
my whole body.
Skin is my body's
biggest organ.

Skin keeps my body

at the right temperature.

My skin sweats to stay cool.

Healthy Skin

I keep my skin healthy

by keeping it clean.

I take baths or showers.

I wash my face.

The sun can burn my skin.

I wear sunscreen

on my face and body.

Cold weather can freeze
my skin.
I wear boots, mittens,
and warm clothes.

I wear bandages
on scrapes and cuts.

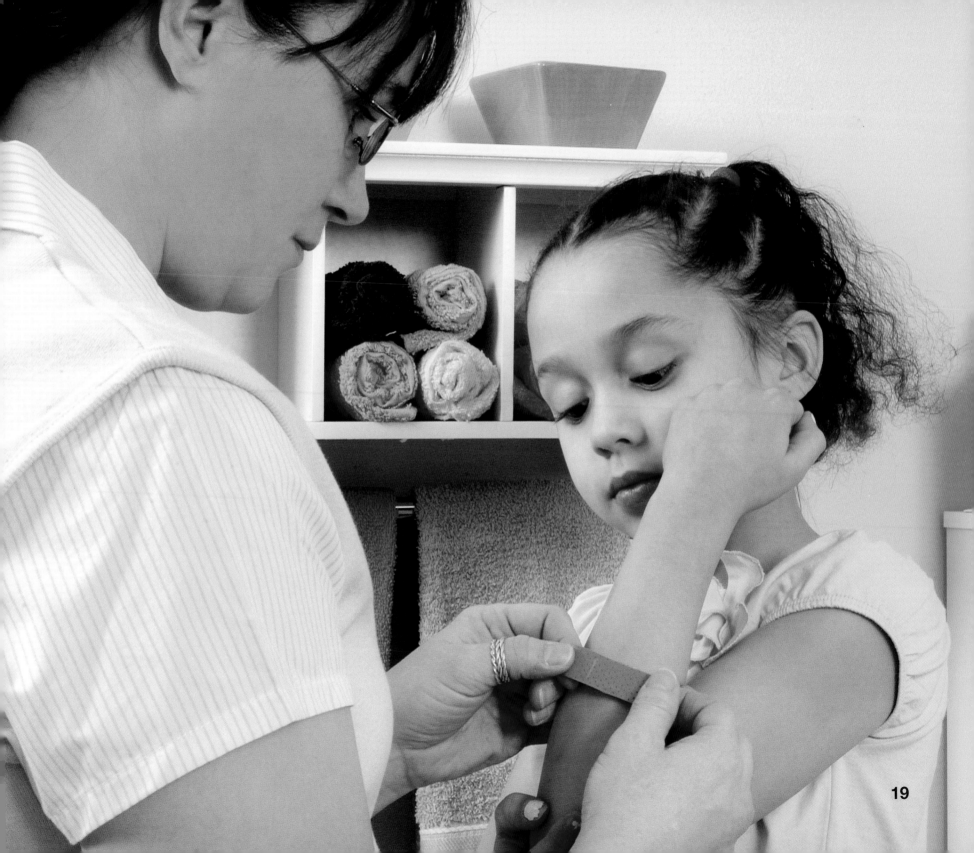

Taking care of my skin

helps keep it healthy.

21

Glossary

brain—the body part inside your head that controls your body; your brain understands what skin touches.

nerve—a bundle of thin fibers that sends messages between your brain and other parts of your body

organ—a part of the body that does a job

temperature—how hot or cold something is

touch—to feel things with your fingers or other parts of your body

Read More

Gordon, Sharon. *Sunburn.* Rookie Read-About Health. Danbury, Conn.: Children's Press, 2002.

Royston, Angela. *Why Do I Get A Sunburn?: And Other Questions About Skin.* Body Matters. Chicago: Heinemann, 2003.

Salzmann, Mary Elizabeth. *Keeping Your Body Clean.* Healthy Habits. Edina, Minn.: Abdo, 2004.

Internet Sites

FactHound offers a safe, fun way to find Internet sites related to this book. All of the sites on FactHound have been researched by our staff.

Here's how:

1. Visit *www.facthound.com*

2. Type in this special code **0736842632** for age-appropriate sites. Or enter a search word related to this book for a more general search.

3. Click on the **Fetch It** button.

FactHound will fetch the best sites for you!

Index

Word Count: 114
Grade: 1
Early-Intervention Level: 15

24